Table of Conte

Foreword

Whether you're looking to try veganism and fasting for weight-loss or you're a vegan wondering about whether intermittent fasting could help improve your health, this book is sure to provide some helpful insights. This book goes into the intricacies of combining a vegan diet with intermittent fasting.

As a bit of in introduction, I have been vegan for 9 years and while I have been thriving on the vegan diet and my health has been excellent, I found myself wondering about the benefits intermittent fasting could bring to my vegan lifestyle.

This book provides a lot of information and goes into great detail on the topics related to both veganism and intermittent fasting, containing helpful information for both seasoned campaigners and beginners alike.

A lot of time was spent researching these topics and I personally tested the methods in the chapters that follow, so you can be sure that this book will give you the insights you need.

I really hope you enjoy the book. Go ahead and get started reading and improving your health and life through veganism and intermittent fasting today!

Chapter One: Basics Of The Vegan Diet

If you've never followed a vegan diet before, you may not be familiar with what it entails and the principles behind it. In essence, a vegan diet avoids all animal products, in lieu of foods derived from fruits, vegetables, seeds, nuts, grains, and other nutrients from the earth.

Reasons People Choose a Vegan Diet

Vegan diets are popular today for a host of reasons:

- Veganism does not harm animals.
- Eating plant-based foods is better for the environment and the planet.
- Vegans typically spend less at the grocery store.
- You can grow your own primary food sources as a vegan.
- A vegan diet may help reverse or lessen the effects of certain conditions and may provide relief from some digestive ailments.
- Many people lose weight and report having more energy when practicing veganism.

Foods Not Permitted on a Vegan Diet

It may surprise you to learn that, in addition to meat, poultry, and fish, there are other foods not allowed on a vegan diet. These include all dairy products, eggs, and even honey for most vegans. In this way, veganism is different from vegetarianism, which does permit dairy, eggs, and honey.

Vegans believe that these animal products are not beneficial or necessary for the body, and many think they are also unethical because of the way animals are treated in their production. The simple act of removing honey from a beehive, for example, disturbs the bees, disrupts their habitat, and deprives them of a winter food source.

Foods Encouraged on a Vegan Diet

Fortunately, the earth provides vegan dieters with an enormous range of foods they can eat. Typical vegan meals are composed of vegetables, fruits, legumes and the like to provide flavour, variety, and nutritive value. Popular vegan staples include:

- seeds, nuts, and nut butters
- tofu, seitan, and tempeh

- plant-based milks and yogurts
- algae and seaweed
- fermented and sprouted foods
- grains and cereals
- legumes (beans and peas)
- fruits and vegetables

There are various versions of the vegan diet that further define eating habits for different personal needs. Some vegans enjoy eating only raw foods, which means nothing is cooked over 118 degrees Fahrenheit. A variation on this diet is eating raw foods until around four o'clock in the afternoon, after which time a regular cooked vegan meal can be consumed. Other vegan subcategories include eating mainly starches and eating mostly low-fat plant-based foods.

History and Culture of Veganism

It is unknown how long people have been practicing intentional veganism, but it is thought to go back thousands of years to the dawn of Hinduism. People of Hindu faith, to this day, do not eat meat. There are other references to abstaining from animal products throughout history, including in the Book of Genesis in the Bible.

Modern veganism began in the mid 19th Century in England and has gathered an enormous following since then. Once labelled a 'hippie' diet from the 1960's, veganism is a now a way of life for many, whether it's because they wish to avoid exploiting animals or simply like how much better they feel when avoiding animal products on the dining room table.

The Science Behind the Vegan Diet

The vegan diet has been studied exhaustively by the medical community, seeing it as a possible cure for diseases that commonly plague society. In addition to lowering the risk of certain types of cancer, heart disease, and diabetes, a vegan diet can reduce arthritis symptoms and lower obesity. A recent study by Oxford University maintains that eating a vegan diet could cut roughly eight million deaths per year, both by improving personal nutrition and by reducing greenhouse emissions caused by raising livestock for food. Far from being a fad diet without scientific support, veganism comes recommended by researchers and nutritionists, and its benefits far outweigh any inconveniences experienced.

Chapter Summary

Key takeaways from this chapter are:

- The vegan diet means eating *no* animal products, including eggs, dairy, and honey.
- There are lots of great plant-based options to provide flavour and nutrition to a vegan diet.
- People choose to follow a vegan diet for a variety of reasons, including health benefits and animal treatment ethics.
- Veganism has been around a long time, and it is scientifically well studied.

In the next chapter you will learn how to ensure adequate protein consumption while on a vegan diet.

Chapter Two: Where Vegans Get Nutrients

Vegan diets that contain a range of natural foods, lots of fruits and vegetables, and a minimum of processed foods provide plenty of vitamins and minerals. However, one of the biggest concerns for vegan dieters is getting enough protein, since animal products, which are typically high-protein sources, are not consumed. Let's take a look at some top vegan protein sources and why they are so important to your nutrition.

How Much Protein Do You Need?

In spite of the popularity of high-protein diets these days, the average person doesn't need to eat a ton of protein to stay healthy and active. It is recommended to eat about 0.36 grams of protein for every pound you weigh, and slightly more is suggested for vegans because of the nature of plant proteins--about 0.41 grams per pound of weight. That works out to about 51 grams of protein per day for a 125-pound person or 74 grams of protein for someone weighing 180 pounds.

How do you know how much protein you are consuming? Packaged foods contain the amount of protein per serving on the label, so you just need to know how many servings you are eating at a time to calculate the protein included. When preparing raw, bulk, or unpackaged foods at home, simply use a nutritionist's food chart to see how much protein you are getting from your groceries.

What Is Protein Anyway?

Proteins are compounds found in nature and are made up of long chains of amino acids (nature's building blocks). You need protein to maintain muscles and to keep your hair, nails, and skin healthy. If you're an athlete, still growing, or a pregnant woman, your protein needs may be higher than those of others because of greater demands on the body.

There are 20 different amino acids that can be combined to form proteins, but nine of those 20 cannot be made by the body. These are commonly called 'essential amino acids'.

Types of Protein

Without these essential amino acids, a protein is not considered 'complete', that is, it won't be as effective in helping you stay healthy and energized.

Meat and eggs are complete proteins in and of themselves. So are quinoa, soy, and buckwheat. However, many plant-based foods are not complete proteins. How do vegans get around this and ensure they get enough complete protein every day? By combining foods to get the right mix of amino acids, thereby creating complete proteins.

Vegan Sources of Protein

It's actually easy to get complete proteins while on a vegan diet because the foods that combine to make them tend to go well together. Classic examples of vegan complete protein combos include:

- hummus and pita bread
- rice and beans
- grains or nuts added to spirulina (a member of the algae family)
- peanut butter on wheat bread
- lentils and corn or lentils and barley (such as in soup or chili)

Other sources of protein that are ideal to incorporate into a vegan diet are:

- chia seeds
- hemp seeds
- pumpkin seeds
- Ezekiel bread
- seitan, tofu, and tempeh
- nuts and nut butters
- veggie burgers and hotdogs
- soy or other veggie crumbles

Are you worried that all this protein combining is starting to sound too complicated? Many vegans find that if they eat a wide variety of foods every day, they don't really need to worry about combining proteins in a formal way because it happens naturally through their food selection. In general, if you eat the foods on the lists above, you should find you are getting adequate protein. One way to check is to keep a log for a week or so to see that you have enough diversity in your vegan diet.

Vegan Substitutions

One aspect of vegan dieting that some people find challenging is not replacing meat at meals but eliminating animal products in other places, like dairy and eggs in baking or recipe ingredients. In addition to vegan cheeses made from nuts, you can use things like applesauce, chia seeds, tofu, mashed banana, ground flaxseed, and arrowroot powder in your baked goods and casseroles.

Chapter Summary

This chapter discussed how to incorporate protein into a vegan diet without eating animal products. Important points to remember include:

- Protein is a necessary dietary component for your body's optimum function.
- There are different types of protein, and it's desirable to eat complete proteins as a regular part of your diet.
- You don't need to eat animal products to get plenty of protein in your diet.
- There are tons of protein sources available to vegans that taste great.

The next chapter takes a look at the basics of intermittent fasting.

Chapter Three: What Is Intermittent Fasting?

You have probably heard of fasting, which is abstaining from food. You may have had to fast before surgery or blood tests at the doctor's office. Some people also fast for religious reasons. Intermittent fasting is going without eating for a set period of time at regular intervals; hence, you fast intermittently. Unlike most diets that are concerned with *what* you eat, intermittent fasting is all about *when* you eat. You'll read why that's so important in the next chapter.

Intermittent fasting is embraced for a number of reasons, some of which will be discussed in subsequent chapters. One of the most popular motivations for intermittent fasting is weight loss, although intermittent fasting can also be done to help with various health issues, to feel less bogged down by food, and even to live longer.

Different Types of Intermittent Fasting

Just like with the vegan diet, there are subtle variations within intermittent fasting too. One common intermittent fasting schedule is known as '16:8' because you fast for 16 hours and then eat within an eight-hour window every day. Another top intermittent fasting plan is the '5:2' diet, which entails eating normally for five days out of the week and then radically restricting calories to about 500 per day for two days per week. Some people fast every other day, alternating with eating normally on other days.

One of the most appealing aspects of intermittent fasting, as you have probably noticed, is that it can be adjusted to meet your personal needs. In addition to a rotating day type of fasting plan, you can also fast every day and manipulate your eating window to best work with your unique schedule. if you're an early riser, you may want to have your first meal by 10 am, eat between 10 and 6 pm, and then fast from 6 pm until 10 am. But if you're more of a night owl, you can start eating at noon and push your fast off until 8 pm.

The Advantages of Intermittent Fasting Over Other Eating Plans

There are literally hundreds, if not thousands, of diets available today. What makes intermittent fasting so much better than most of them?

- You can start immediately, with no big shopping lists to complete first.

- You will spend less money, not more, because you'll be eating less often.
- You can adapt the fasting schedule to suit your lifestyle, so if you work nights, for example, you simply shift your fasting time to when you're awake in the evening.
- You can rest assured that intermittent fasting is not a fad; it has been practiced in some form or another for centuries, and it is very well studied clinically.
- You don't have to join any plans, purchase scales, or buy special diet food items.
- You can skip a day occasionally for a special holiday meal or event and get right back into your fasting schedule with ease.
- You don't have to worry about toting diet meals to work or bringing your own food to a restaurant because of severe diet restrictions.
- You don't have to deprive yourself of your favourite foods or eat foods you don't like.

Chapter Summary

Here are the most important things to remember about intermittent fasting.

- Intermittent fasting is the practice of going without food at regular intervals.
- You can fast intermittently every day, every other day, or a few times per week.
- Intermittent fasting has lots of compelling reasons for its current popularity, especially ease of starting and flexibility.

Keep reading because the next chapter is all about the health benefits of intermittent fasting.

Chapter Four: Health Benefits Of Intermittent Fasting

Intermittent fasting has been well studied by doctors and dietitians and found to have numerous health benefits. But before you learn about all those advantages, it's important to understand exactly how intermittent fasting works.

The Effects of Intermittent Fasting on the Body

When you eat any sugars that your body doesn't use right away, they are stored in your cells as fat. Insulin, a hormone produced by the body to help it use sugar properly, is the freight train that carries sugar to the cells for storage. When you eat all day long, especially a diet high in carbohydrates, your insulin keeps getting spiked, causing you not only to gain weight but to eventually lose sensitivity to insulin itself.

Whenever your insulin levels go down, the body recognizes there's no immediate sugar to be used as fuel, so it releases fat from where it has been stored in the cells to give you energy. One way to induce your insulin levels to decline naturally is to stop eating. This helps you lose weight by burning fat.

Fasting is a reliable way to repeatedly reduce the insulin in your bloodstream. If you fast regularly, over time your body becomes better at regulating and using insulin, known as improving insulin sensitivity.

What Else Can Intermittent Fasting Do?

While people have been fasting for centuries, including intermittent fasting (whether accidentally or intentionally), this method of eating didn't come under the scrutiny of medical researchers until the 1930's. Doctors at Cornell University discovered that rats that ate less lived longer. Fifteen years later, researchers at the University of Chicago revealed that alternate-day feeding had the same effect.

More recent studies on animal models have demonstrated that intermittent fasting can slow down or protect participants from:

- damage from strokes
- Alzheimer's disease

- Parkinson's disease
- cognitive decline

Why Intermittent Fasting Is So Successful Now

Let's go back to the basics of intermittent fasting for a moment to see why this way of eating is so popular today. Obesity and diabetes/pre-diabetes are an epidemic in the Western world, particularly in the United States. A well-studied dietary regimen that allows people to improve their sensitivity to insulin, prevent diabetes, reduce the severity of diabetes, and lose weight, like intermittent fasting does, makes sense.

Many people have lost the ability to know when they really need to eat. Intermittent fasting restores that by at first restricting your eating hours and then by helping the body's hormones tell you when it needs fuel. People who follow intermittent fasting programs report no longer being hungry all day long, reduced unnecessary snacking, and a return of normal hunger pangs only when they should eat (more on this in Chapter Twelve).

Chapter Summary

This was an important chapter, so take a moment to revisit the health benefits.

Intermittent fasting:

- has been well researched for its health benefits.
- lets you burn fat when you're not eating.
- can help stabilize insulin and prevent the progression of diabetes.
- helps the body return to normal hunger cues.
- in animal models shows far-ranging benefits related to brain function and longevity.

The next chapter in this book discusses even more health benefits of intermittent fasting and how it can even have a healing effect on the body.

Chapter Five: Healing Powers Of Intermittent Fasting

In Chapter Four, you learned about the health benefits of intermittent fasting. But did you know there are even more advantages to this eating plan that may involve healing the body?

A Review of Insulin and Intermittent Fasting

You just read about how intermittent fasting helps your body use and respond to insulin more subtly, but it's worth repeating here when discussing the healing powers of intermittent fasting. Improving insulin sensitivity doesn't just help you lose weight, which can be a great benefit on its own; it can prevent prediabetes from progressing to full-blown diabetes. In some cases, intermittent fasting can even reduce the severity of Type 2 diabetes, when practiced under the care of a physician. Those healing effects alone make intermittent fasting worth considering for many people.

Inflammatory Healing with Intermittent Fasting

Increasing insulin sensitivity is just the proverbial tip of the iceberg when it comes to the physiological healing that's possible with intermittent fasting. One of the other great benefits of this eating regimen is its ability to ease inflammation for some people. Studies on intermittent fasting show it can reduce inflammatory markers--biological signs that show up in blood tests-- for a range of inflammation, including arthritis and even asthma symptoms.

Why is healing inflammation so important? Not only does reducing inflammation potentially alleviate pain, it also reduces the risk of high blood pressure and cardiac disease. Intermittent fasting is doubly helpful with regard to blood pressure because it can decrease inflammation and at the same time directly lower blood pressure as well.

Digestion and Intermittent Fasting

One place in the body where many people experience inflammation, often without even knowing it, is in the digestive system. We have both beneficial and not-so-helpful bacteria (flora) in our gut that can fall out of balance with the wrong diet and by constant eating. Some flora may even work their way into the bloodstream through microscopic tears in the digestive tract (known as 'leaky gut syndrome').

Intermittent fasting allows the gut flora to rebalance itself because you're not constantly filling the digestive tract with food and asking it to work. Normal digestive enzymes, hormones, and other chemical compounds can finally settle into a more natural state.

Other Healing Benefits of Intermittent Fasting

The ability of the body to rest when not eating cannot be underestimated with intermittent fasting. When you eat, you not only stress your digestive system but your entire body. Blood is shunted from other areas of the body to the stomach and intestines to process food. (Remember the old adage about not swimming right after eating? That's why.) Sleep may be disrupted if you're trying to digest food too late at night. Vital cells that are needed for healing are slowed down to make way for digestion.

It's good to give your body a break from constantly trying to process food. Think of it like shutting down the assembly line in a factory to allow the machinery to cool off and prevent wear and tear. This is especially true if your body requires serious healing for a condition or injury, such as a recent surgery, a sports trauma, or a serious bout of the flu.

This also holds true for chronic illnesses, like thyroid disease, adrenal insufficiency, and fibromyalgia. You may find that once you have practiced intermittent fasting for a while, the symptoms of long-term conditions improve and you have more energy because your body is not being over tasked with too many functions.

Chapter Summary

In this chapter we looked at the healing powers of intermittent fasting.

- Intermittent fasting can help reduce inflammation, which not only relieves pain but may benefit long-term cardiovascular health.
- It can also reduce gut inflammation and help restore digestive health.
- Intermittent fasting also gives your body a break from processing food so it can devote its energy to other functions.

In the next chapter you will learn about the pillars of intermittent fasting that you need to know to be successful with this type of eating regimen.

Chapter Six: Pillars Of Intermittent Fasting

By now you should know quite a bit more about intermittent fasting than you did when you started this book. Here are some key points that have been touched on and for which you will receive gentle reminders throughout the rest of the book, the 'rules' of intermittent fasting, if you will.

1. Choose an intermittent fasting schedule that you can realistically sustain. You may think fasting for 20 hours per day will help you achieve results faster, but if you can't do this for more than a few days, you will only wind up quitting before you see any benefits. Instead, pick a plan that works for your schedule and ramp up to your desired fasting time by incrementally reducing your eating window (see Chapter Ten).

2. Do not eat anything during the time you are supposed to be fasting. You are allowed to drink as much water, tea, black coffee, and diet soda as you like during your fast times. Stay hydrated by quenching your thirst with water and herbal tea. If possible, avoid diet soda, which some studies show may make you want to pig out when you do finally get to eat.

3. Do not overeat when your fast time is up. Technically, you can eat what you want when you're not fasting, but gorging will have multiple negative effects. If you are trying to lose weight, eating too many calories, even with fasting, may keep you from dropping pounds. Also, overeating taxes your digestive system, which is one of the things you are trying to avoid with intermittent fasting.

4. Spread your eating out over your non-fasting window, especially if you are fasting for a portion of every day. While you can fast for most of the day and eat one meal per day, you may feel less cranky and have more energy if you eat several times within your eating window. As mentioned above, you don't want to overeat with intermittent fasting, and eating only once per day may unwittingly encourage that.

5. Eat a range of vegan foods when you are not fasting, so you are sure to get the protein, vitamins, and minerals you need. Avoid junk food, even if it doesn't contain animal products.

6. See a doctor if you have any concerns about whether or not intermittent fasting is for you. Contraindications (reasons to avoid) to fasting are listed in Chapter Thirteen, but you may have questions that only your personal healthcare provider can answer.

7. Stop fasting or reduce your fasting time if you experience any of the following:

- light-headedness
- dizziness
- fainting spells
- nausea
- blurred vision
- weakness
- extreme fatigue
- inability to sleep

Chapter Summary

This chapter reviewed the 'rules' for intermittent fasting. Go over them a few times before you start to make sure you understand how to fast.

- Pick a realistic schedule for fasting.
- Don't eat food during your fasting window.
- Don't overeat during your designated eating times.
- Know the signs that tell you to slow down or reduce your fasting time.

You've learned about both veganism and intermittent fasting so far. The next chapter will show you how to combine the two.

Chapter Seven: Combining Veganism and Intermittent Fasting

Mixing a vegan diet and intermittent fasting sounds like a giant task, but it's really quite a fantastic pairing if you approach it right. This chapter will give you some tips for combining the two.

Advantages of Veganism During Intermittent Fasting

One of the biggest challenges faced by anyone doing intermittent fasting is hunger pangs. That hunger will rear its angry head faster if the food you consume during your eating window is digested quickly. The more refined a food is the faster your body processes it.

Fortunately, natural vegan food (not vegan junk food--yes, there is such a thing!) is generally high in fibre, whether you're eating legumes, vegetables or fruits. So, one big key to feeling full longer is to keep eating lots of fibre and to eat it throughout the periods when you are allowed to eat.

Other foods that are vegan staples also help keep your stomach from grumbling. Fats take longer to digest than carbohydrates, so be sure to add some to your diet.

Foods to Stay Satiated

If you're heading to the grocery store and want to purchase some foods that make you feel satiated, here's a great list to start with:

- legumes (beans, lentils, peas, chickpeas, etc.)
- leafy greens (lettuce, spinach, kale, etc.)
- cruciferous veggies (broccoli, cauliflower, etc.)
- fruits and vegetables with the peel intact (apples, peppers, pears, etc.)
- nuts, nut butters, and seeds
- olives and olive oil
- avocados
- squash and pumpkin
- berries and fruits/vegetables with seeds (pomegranates, cucumbers, etc.)
- fibrous vegetables (celery, asparagus, green beans, etc.)
- whole grains and whole grain products (pasta, cereal, bread)

- dried fruits and raisins
- hemp products
- dates and figs
- veggie burgers and veggie crumbles
- vegan 'cheese' made from nuts
- edamame (soybeans)

Chapter Summary

Combining a vegan diet with intermittent fasting is easy and natural.

- Eat high-fibre foods, which are staples of the vegan kitchen, to stay feeling full longer.
- High-fat vegan foods also keep you feeling satiated.

In the next chapter you will learn some advice for starting a new diet.

Chapter Eight: How, When And Where To Start

The beauty of a vegan intermittent fasting regimen is you can start virtually anywhere, any time. There are a few tips, however, that will make commencing your new eating plan go much more smoothly.

Go at Your Own Pace

If you are starting both a vegan diet and intermittent fasting at the same time, you may feel overwhelmed with so much change happening at once. Instead, before trying intermittent fasting, try the vegan diet for a few weeks or so. You will be less likely to chuck it all in out of frustration if you have one aspect of your new eating plan under your belt before adding another.

If you are going from being a full-on carnivore to vegan, you may want to take even more time. Start by weaving meatless meals into your weekly menu. Then, stop eating meat, fish, and poultry. Finally, eliminate other animal products like dairy and eggs to complete the transition.

Likewise, you can ramp up your intermittent fasting schedule so it's not a total shock to your body all at once (see Chapter Ten). Let's say you've decided to follow a plan that allows for eight hours of eating followed by 16 hours of fasting. You may be ravenous when you first start fasting, to the point where you give up on the diet before you have a chance to reap its benefits. Rather than psyching yourself out, try fasting for 10 hours first, then 12, then 14, and finally 16.

Take a Look at Your Calendar

While you can certainly start a vegan intermittent fasting plan today if you like, you may want to check your calendar first to make sure it's the ideal time to increase your chances for success. If you are heading to a wedding on the coming weekend, taking a vacation with the family, or running your first marathon, it may not be the time to utterly revamp your diet. Look for a time when life is relatively calm, so you won't have any hurdles that make the change next to impossible.

Map Out a Plan of Action

Whenever you start a new eating regimen, you want to have a plan in place before you begin. Think of it like a roadmap to a new destination when driving your car.

Take a realistic look at your daily schedule to decide when it's best to fast and when it's best to eat. Build in cooking prep time, so you won't sabotage yourself with junk food or resort to grabbing a burger when you're starving.

Enlist a Support Team

Making big dietary changes is challenging. Be aware that some people will be enthusiastic cheerleaders for you, while others may resent your foray into better health. Ignore the naysayers, and focus on people who will support you in your endeavour.

There are lots of places to find people who will aid you in your new eating adventure or even join you in vegan intermittent fasting:

- the gym or health club
- running, cycling, and triathlon training groups
- the office or workplace
- online chat groups and forums
- organic and health food stores
- local produce growers, community supported agriculture, and farmer's markets
- vegan restaurants
- cooking groups and courses
- organizations and clubs where you are a member

Set Yourself Up for Success

Don't forget to become your own biggest cheerleader! You know yourself better than anyone else--your strengths and your weaknesses. Try to anticipate places where you might run into trouble, and head them off at the pass. For example, if you are trying not to eat until 10 am but breakfast is a temptation, indulge in some gourmet brewed black coffee to reward yourself and stave off diet sabotage.

You can also leave messages around the house to remind you why you're making changes to your diet. Pin them to the fridge, the bathroom mirror, and the dashboard of your car for extra motivation throughout the day.

Keeping a log or journal is also a great way to stay on track. Not only can you write about any hurdles to get them out of your system, you can also create a visual reminder of your progress to see how far you've come and mark your victories.

Be Ready for Failure

Yes, you read that line right. Be ready for failure. Why? Because when making any major changes to your life, you may trip up once in a while. If you anticipate this and have a plan ready to get back in the game, any deviations from your intermittent fasting plan or vegan diet will just be blips on the larger screen of success.

Remind yourself that even sports legends and Olympic athletes sometimes fail to reach their goals on the first try. Do they give up? Of course not, and neither should you if you falter. Think of any goofs as one-offs, and go right back to your eating plan, which is easy with intermittent fasting.

Chapter Summary

Starting intermittent fasting as a vegan is simple, especially if you know a few top tips for success.

- Plan well in advance and pick a low-stress time to start.
- Get support for your efforts and tune out naysayers.
- Break your new life change into manageable chunks as needed; start by going vegan first, then add intermittent fasting.

In the next chapter you will learn about exercising while fasting.

Chapter Nine: Exercise And Working Out While Fasting

One of the most common questions posed by new intermittent fasters is "How do I exercise or work out while I'm fasting?" Surprisingly, many people actually have more energy and feel better when they fast, so working out isn't an issue. But if you're someone who is concerned about "bonking" during your workout, read on to learn some suggestions for keeping your energy up.

Timing Your Workouts

One of the biggest worries when exercising in combination with intermittent fasting is how to time your workouts. In many ways, the answer is a personal one that depends on your metabolism, your unique body chemistry, and the type and intensity of exercise you perform.

Most athletes have to experiment a bit to find a schedule that works best for them. In general, if you're not working out hard, you have more leeway in timing your exercise sessions. Light exercise means less demand on the muscles and less competition between the digestive system and the musculoskeletal system.

If you up the intensity of your sport, however, you will likely need to give more thought to when to exercise in relation to eating. If you are trying to lose weight through exercise and fasting, it's best if you can exercise right before eating at the end of a fasting period, as long as you can do it without losing your energy. Exercise gives your metabolism a boost for a few hours afterward, so when you reward yourself with a post-workout meal, your body is still in calorie burning mode. This schedule is ideal for morning exercisers.

However, if you can't make it through a workout without feeling fatigued, or if lack of stamina is affecting the quality of your performance, you may need to exercise during an eating window or within a few hours of eating. Are you an evening exerciser? This schedule may work better for you. Just make sure you have digested your food for about an hour or two before working out. Also, try to split up your eating, so you're not exercising after one huge meal.

Nutritional Needs and Exercise

The intensity of your exercise, coupled with your own physiology, determines how much and what type of food you need to eat to stoke your body's engines when working out. Also, your desire to lose or maintain weight figures into your menu.

As you've already learned, a vegan diet can provide plenty of protein as well as food that keeps you full all day. You may want to go up a bit on the protein if you're training super hard, such as for a marathon or triathlon, or if you are trying to increase muscle mass (muscle is built on protein). You also want to eat as well-rounded a diet as possible, so you get all the nutrients you need. If you feel you are missing vitamins and minerals from your diet, you can add over-the counter supplements to fill in.

Exercising and Losing Weight While Fasting

One of the boons of intermittent fasting is that you can lose weight fairly easily without limiting calories, simply by observing your fasting schedule and not overeating during your food windows. While weight loss is enhanced by exercise, even when practicing intermittent fasting, know that you can ease up a bit on the workouts if you are already losing weight through fasting. Instead of forcing yourself to do exhausting cardio for hours, you can enjoy other forms of exercise for fitness, like:

- tai chi or soft martial arts
- dancing
- softball
- swimming
- walking or light jogging
- Pilates
- yoga
- recreational cycling
- golfing
- light resistance work
- gardening and housework

Additional Tips for Working Out and Intermittent Fasting

Working out while practicing intermittent fasting should be fun and rewarding. Once you figure out the perfect schedule for you, use these tips for improved performance:

1. Stay hydrated. Drinking plenty of water throughout the day will help you to feel full and make you less likely to cheat by eating when you shouldn't. Water is essential to keep your muscles and joints functioning at an optimum level. And water also helps your body remove toxins and waste through the urinary and digestive systems. You'll process and absorb nutrients better when you're thoroughly hydrated.

2. Try a little caffeine before working out. Studies show that a small amount of caffeine, such as the amount in a cup of black coffee, taken right before exercise can increase the uptake of free fatty acids in the bloodstream. What does that mean? Caffeine can help you burn fat instead of glycogen (sugar-based fuel) during exercise.

3. Have some food prepped for immediately after exercise if that's when you're scheduled to eat. Particularly if you are making recipes from scratch at home, you need to do a little work in advance to make sure you have healthy foods available to you. Take a cooked sweet potato, a container of berries, or a handful of nuts with you to the gym if you have a long ride home after working out. Otherwise, you may succumb to the temptation of junk food when you're starving and pressed for time.

4. If you're worried you're not getting enough nutrients for your workout routine, consult your physician, or a professional dietician or trainer experienced with vegan diets and intermittent fasting.

5. If you feel the need for a cardio burn, but don't want to devote an hour or more every day to running or similar exercise, try HIIT or high-intensity interval training. HIIT typically entails doing short bursts of aerobic exercise, interspersed with recovery periods, for about 30 minutes. Many fans of intermittent fasting report HIIT suits them very well and adds a bit of oomph to their weight loss efforts.

Chapter Summary

Exercising or working out can be combined with intermittent fasting, but it just takes a little thought, and sometimes trial and error, to make it work for you.

- Find the right time to exercise based on your unique needs and eating schedule.
- Make sure you are eating healthy vegan foods to meet all your nutritional needs.
- Because you may already be losing weight with intermittent fasting, you can usually lighten up on the cardio workouts and have fun with other types of exercise for strength and flexibility.
- Prepare in advance: have water and healthy foods ready at all times.
- A little caffeine consumed before exercise can help you burn fat instead of glycogen. Fat is a more efficient source of fuel; save the glycogen for your brain!

The next chapter gets into the nuts and bolts of intermittent fasting by offering you a sample fasting plan you can start as soon as now.

Chapter Ten: Simple Fasting Plan

Do you need a little more help getting started with an intermittent fasting plan? Here is a plan to begin fasting that starts out easy and ramps up gradually over the course of three to four weeks to a longer fasting window. Don't forget, it's perfectly fine to go at your own pace. If you're not ready for a longer fast, stay where you are for a bit longer.

An Intermittent Fasting Plan You Can Start Today (16:8 Fasting)

Week One:

- Eat between 7am and 7pm (12 hours)
- Fast between 7pm and 7am (12 hours)

This schedule of 12 hours on/12 hours off gets you used to eating within set times and starts getting you into the mind-set of fasting, so you're paying more attention to when you eat and your body's hunger cues. You'll notice that it capitalizes on your circadian rhythm (your body's natural timetable that revolves around sunrise and sunset). Additionally, this plan gives you a few hours after your last meal before bed. Numerous studies demonstrate that eating too close to sleep increases the risk of diabetes and obesity.

If you work nights or swing shifts, you will obviously have to adjust this fasting plan, but if you normally work during the day, it's best if you can take advantage of your body's natural fasting time during sleep at night.

Week Two:

- Eat between 8am and 6pm (10 hours)
- Fast between 6pm and 8am (14 hours)

You'll note that this week, you're adding two hours to your fast time.

Week Three:

- Eat between 10am and 6pm (8 hours)
- Fast between 6pm and 10am (16 hours)

The third week of your intermittent fasting plan adds another two hours to your fast window. You have now reached the 16:8 daily fasting schedule. Even though you are technically fasting for 16 hours per day, about seven or eight hours of that time is spent sleeping, so a good chunk of your abstinence from food will pass quickly.

If this schedule doesn't work with your job, exercise, family, or social schedules, simply adjust it. You can still fast for 16 hours by eating from 11am until 7pm, for example. Just make sure the ratio of eating to fasting time stays the same.

Week Four (Optional):

- Eat between 12 noon and 6pm (6 hours)
- Fast between 6pm and 12 noon (18 hours)

Fasting for 18 hours may be more than most people can handle, and it's definitely something you need to work up to slowly. But the extra fast time can benefit people who want to lose weight by intermittent fasting. If you try the Week Four schedule and find it's too much for you, go back to Week Three and stay there.

Alternative Fasting Plans

Here are two fasting plans for people who don't want to fast every day. Maybe you know yourself well enough to know that you won't stick to a daily plan. Perhaps you have an active social life and want to make sure you can still go out with friends. Each of these two alternate plans will let you accommodate those needs. The best intermittent fasting plan is the one you can stay with long term and fashion into a lifestyle!

Alternative Plan #1 (5:2 Fasting):

- Eat normally, consuming a healthy vegan diet on Monday, Wednesday, Thursday, Saturday, and Sunday.
- Fast on Tuesday and Friday, eating no more than 500 calories on each of those days.

You'll see this plan doesn't involve any mandatory times for completely going without food, other than when you're sleeping. However, if you eat one or two small meals that total 500 calories within a small window of time, your fasting days will be similar to the fasting windows observed during the 16:8 plan reached by Week Three above.

You can shift this schedule to any 5:2 ratio during the week. Just make sure that your two fasting days are non-consecutive days of the week (not two days in a row). You can actually eat quite a lot of food on a vegan diet and still only consume 500 calories. The foods below are easy to eat in small portions and can be prepared to give you adequate vitamins and protein.

Suggested foods for your 500-calorie days include:

- vegan yogurt
- hummus and vegetables
- legume soup
- salads
- cereal and grains
- nuts

Alternative Plan #2 (Alternate-Day Fasting):

- Eat normally on Monday, Wednesday, Friday, Sunday.
- Fast on Tuesday, Thursday, and Saturday.

This plan will create a rolling schedule, where one week you are fasting on Tuesday, Thursday, and Saturday and the next week you are fasting on opposite days. The idea is to constantly alternate your fast days with your normal eating days. Some people like to eat nothing on their fast days. But most people find this very difficult, so they eat 500 calories on their fast days.

Chapter Summary

You can start intermittent fasting today with any of the plans outlined above.

- Plan #1, the most common, lets you eat for eight hours per day, and then you fast for 16 hours. This plan is practiced every day of the week.
- Plan #2 lets you eat normally for five days of the week, and you fast on two days by eating only 500 calories per day. This is the best plan for people whose family or social lives revolve around meals or for whom daily fasting may be challenging.
- Plan #3 is an alternate-day fasting schedule, where you eat normally on one day and eat only 500 calories the next.

The next chapter will outline an exercise plan to go with your intermittent fasting diet.

Chapter Eleven: Sample Workout Plan

Are you wondering how to integrate your exercise regimen with intermittent fasting? Have you been a bit of a couch potato recently and want to get back to working out when you start your intermittent fasting plan?

Here is a sample workout plan you can begin right away. Remember from previous chapters that if your main goal with intermittent fasting is to lose weight, you may do that with fasting alone. It's better to combine diet and exercise for weight loss and overall health, but you can cut back on the cardio a little with intermittent fasting and enjoy other types of exercise that aren't so exhausting and hard on the body.

Weekly Exercise Plan

Monday:

- 30 - 50 minutes brisk walking or light jogging
- 5 minutes of crunches and/or planks
- 5 minutes cool down with gentle stretching

Tuesday:

- 20 - 30 minutes HIIT (high-intensity interval training) workout
- 10 minutes cool down with gentle stretching

Wednesday:

- 30 - 60 minutes of any low-impact exercise for joint mobility and flexibility: yoga, Pilates, tai chi, light water exercise/swimming
- (Optional: take this day off if you want two days of rest per week.)

Thursday:

- 30 - 90 minutes of playing a sport: tennis, softball, soccer, fencing, horseback riding, skating, basketball, canoeing, dancing, etc.
- 10 minutes cool down with gentle stretching

Friday:

- 20 - 30 minutes HIIT (high-intensity interval training) workout
- 10 minutes cool down with gentle stretching

Saturday:

- 30 - 60 minutes of any low-impact exercise for joint mobility and flexibility: yoga, Pilates, tai chi, water exercise/swimming
Sunday:

- Day off--no exercise

What's the theory behind this exercise routine? You'll notice it varies high-intensity work with stretching, moderate activity, and sports. This allows your body to recover after heavy workouts.

The variety makes the plan interesting, so you don't get bored doing the same thing day after day. Switching things up keeps your body guessing too, so you're more likely to burn calories with every workout instead of plateauing. By doing a range of different types of exercise, you build strength, maintain cardiovascular health, improve your range of motion, and develop both fine and gross motor skills.

You can obviously change this routine to suit your hobbies and schedule, but if you're at a loss or need some structure, it gives you a place to start. The idea is to alternate heavier and lighter workouts, both in terms of intensity and time, and include some fun, like playing on a team or trying a new sport.

Chapter Summary

While you can lose weight with intermittent fasting alone, it's better to combine it with exercise for overall health and fitness.

- Because intermittent fasting is already helping you burn calories, you can cut some of the cardio workout time from your schedule if you are doing it nearly every day.
- Vary your exercise routines in terms of intensity and time. Alternate heavy workouts with ones that include more stretching and gentle exercise.
- Include a day of fun sport for variety and skill building.

The next chapter will discuss what you can expect when you start intermittent fasting, including both the benefits and challenges you are likely to encounter.

Chapter Twelve: What To Expect And Potential Effects

If you're ready to give intermittent fasting a try, you may be wondering what to expect, both good and bad in the process. Here's a look at some issues intermittent fasters commonly face as well as tips for getting over initial hurdles. Of course, there are also great benefits, so you'll be reminded of those too, lest you forget why you want to make changes to your eating habits.

Adjusting Your Schedule

For most people starting an intermittent fasting regimen, changing their schedule is one of the most challenging aspects. You will likely be adjusting the times you eat, which may mean giving up breakfast with the family or going out for late night dinners with friends. If you lean towards frequent social eating or those family meals are crucial for you, 5:2 fasting or alternate-day fasting are probably best for you. You can get your fasting in and still have days where you can keep your social schedule intact.

Don't forget to look at your sleep schedule too. Especially in the beginning, you may find you need more snooze time than normal, and even once you have acclimated to the diet, you want to make sure you get enough rest. Fasting is a minor, manageable stress on the body, but it can become overwhelming if you are unduly fatigued.

You've already read about possibly needing to adjust your workout schedule too. It's likely you'll need to experiment with a few different eat-fast-exercise configurations to figure out which one works best for you.

Dealing with Hunger Pangs

Another common hurdle new intermittent fasters face is managing hunger. You will feel hungry at times at the start of your new fasting lifestyle, but that usually goes away for the most part. Even so, you will realize that being a little hungry isn't a catastrophe. If you tough it out for a little while, ghrelin (your hunger hormone) recedes on its own.

Sometimes you can confuse hunger with thirst. If you feel hungry, try drinking a large glass of water, or have a cup of coffee or tea. You may find your 'hunger pangs' abate when you quench your thirst.

Eating Strategically

Strategic eating is another way to manage hunger. If you have an eight-hour window in which to eat and you only eat one meal, guess what? You will probably be hungry during part of your fasting time. But if you spread your meals out over the entire eight-hour window, you'll be less likely to experience hunger and you won't run out of energy at work or during exercise.

Enjoying Desirable Results

You just read about how ghrelin, the hormone that tells you you're hungry, comes and goes over time. One of the benefits of intermittent fasting is that your ghrelin sensitivity, in addition to your reaction to insulin, becomes more acute. After practicing intermittent fasting for a month or two, you'll probably notice you're not getting as hungry as you used to. Congratulations, your body is returning to its normal, natural way of being!

You've read about the benefits of intermittent fasting in previous chapters, but let's review them again, as inspiration for when you're first starting out:

- lowers cholesterol
- lowers insulin level in blood
- improves insulin sensitivity
- promotes weight loss
- reduces inflammatory markers
- helps rebalance gut flora
- decreases risk of various brain conditions and cognitive decline
- lowers blood pressure

Chapter Summary

This chapter focused on what to expect when you begin intermittent fasting.

- Expect to have some hunger pangs initially, but they will get better.
- You will have to adjust your schedule somewhat to eat fewer hours of

the day.

- Intermittent fasting offers so many wonderful benefits, you will likely find they outweigh any negative issues.

Only one chapter left! Keep reading for a few final considerations.

Chapter Thirteen: Final Considerations

Before you head off to try intermittent fasting and a vegan diet on your own, there are a few final things to consider and a few reminders worth mentioning.

Weight Loss Maintenance on Intermittent Fasting

If you begin intermittent fasting with the goal of losing weight, you may reach your goal but not desire to drop any more pounds. You want to be careful that you don't fast too much and lose weight you can't afford to part with.

Some people's weight naturally levels off without an adjustment to their intermittent fasting diet. However, if you are worried about continuing to lose after you hit your goal weight, here are a few tips:

- Add some higher calorie foods to your diet. You don't want to go overboard or resort to eating junk food. But an extra avocado, a little more olive oil on your salad, or an extra sweet potato here and there may be just what you need to stop losing and stay at your desired weight.
- Look at your exercise plan. Are you still working out like you need to drop 20 pounds even after you've lost the weight? You can do one of two things: either keep working out hard and increase your caloric input or cut back a little on the exercise. If you're doing a lot of high-intensity or cardio exercise, consider swapping out some hard training days for something more gentle, like yoga, tai chi, or walking.
- Adjust your fasting plan. This is especially true if you are fasting every day with a very small eating window. Some people eat in only a tiny four-hour window for drastic weight loss, but this may not be sustainable once you hit your goal weight. Try lengthening your eating period by an hour or two.

Intermittent Fasting Is Not a Miracle

There is no doubt that intermittent fasting has changed people's lives for the better, whether by improving health conditions or simply making them feel more energetic. However, fasting is not a solution to every health problem, nor does it produce overnight results. You need to first make sure you don't have unrealistic expectations, and you need to give intermittent fasting at least a month of religious practice to see if it works for you. You may feel better right away, but you may also need more time to see anti-inflammatory results, to better regulate your insulin sensitivity, and to restore your normal cues for hunger.

A vegan diet is also not a miracle worker. While eating plant-based foods is a wonderful choice for your overall health, you still can't gorge on whatever you like (an entire pan of vegan brownies) or eat only vegan junk food. The quality and the quantity of the food you eat is vital. Likewise, when eating between fasts with intermittent fasting, you shouldn't be overeating. Moderation in all things related to diet is definitely the way to go.

You Should Not Feel Sick While Fasting

Some people feel better almost immediately when they begin an intermittent fasting plan. However, other people feel tired, cranky, hungry, and generally out of sorts even after a few weeks in. If you find yourself feeling this way, it doesn't necessarily mean intermittent fasting is wrong for you; it could mean you need to tweak your personal program for your individual needs:

- Examine the length of time you are fasting. It could be too long for you. Try shortening your fast time by an hour or two to see if you feel better.
- Your fast window may be fine in terms of length, but you may need to shift it to earlier or later in the day to accommodate your schedule and nutritional needs.
- You may have selected the wrong fasting plan for yourself. For example, you may be practicing daily 16:8 fasting when 5:2 or alternate-day fasting might work better. Try switching plans to see if that has an effect on your mood and health.
- Are you consuming food throughout your entire eating window, or are you stuffing all your eating into one meal? While a few people do well with only eating one meal a day, most people feel better when they can spread their eating out. Try eating two or three smaller meals during your non-fast times to keep up your energy and stave off hunger.
- If you are an exerciser, especially one who trains hard, you may need to adjust your workout time to better suit your new intermittent fasting

plan. You may also need to time your meals differently with your workouts.

- Are you eating high-quality vegan foods? Getting enough protein and other nutrients? Be sure to review the chapters on vegan dieting to see if you can improve your sources of nutrition. Also, even with a healthy diet of natural foods, it's possible to miss some nutrients. Potassium, for example, is a difficult element to consume in sufficient quality through diet alone. You may need a supplement to pick up the slack.
- Don't forget to stay hydrated! Water will help you digest your food and absorb nutrients better and will keep you feeling full longer.
- Are you cheating? Remember, you can only have black coffee, tea, water, or diet soda during your fasts. Nothing else is allowed. Intermittent fasting can't work if you aren't actually fasting!

Contraindications for Intermittent Fasting

Intermittent fasting is safe and effective for most people. If you have doubts about fasting, consult your healthcare provider first. Even though intermittent fasting can mitigate many of the symptoms of diabetes, anyone with Type 2 diabetes should check with a doctor first before trying to fast (and Type 1 diabetics who are insulin dependent should never fast; see below).

There are some people who should not try intermittent or any kind of fasting. If you belong to any of the following categories, you should not fast:

- children
- underweight people
- malnourished people
- people with a history of eating disorders
- people with chronic hypoglycaemia (without physician's consent)
- Type 1 diabetics (and possibly Type 2, depending on doctor's advice)
- pregnant women
- lactating women
- people who need to take medicine throughout the day with food
- people under chronic stress
- individuals suffering from hormone dysregulation (e.g., menopause or hypothyroidism) without regulating hormones first
- anyone who has had a serious negative reaction to fasting in the past

You Can Do It!

Making any big changes in life can be scary and require us to create a different version of ourselves to succeed. But without change, we stagnate and never reach the goals we aspire to, including having a healthier body. Be confident you can change your life. You will find that taking that one step towards improving your diet and wellness will have a ripple effect, and you will be able to then handle other challenges you have been aspiring towards. Onward!

Chapter Summary

Now you have new insight into both the vegan diet and intermittent fasting, and it's time to try it yourself.

- Review the contraindications for intermittent fasting, and make sure it's right for you.
- Be realistic about your goals and give the plan time to work.
- Be flexible, and be ready to make adjustments to an intermittent fasting lifestyle to suit your personal needs.
- Use small tweaks to adjust your intermittent fasting plan if you are using fasting to lose weight and don't want to keep losing after you hit that magic number on the scale.
- Have confidence in your ability to change, and not only will you improve your health, you'll open the door to reaching other life goals you've always wanted to achieve!

Final Words

So there we have it, I really hope that this book has provided you with the insight and knowledge you were looking for.

Whether you're a vegan like me or simply curious about trying something a little different, combining veganism and fasting can really be a match made in heaven. The health benefits to be derived from combining the two can be tremendous! Intermittent fasting and veganism can indeed work very well together, and perform wonders for your health and wellness.

One of the major upsides is that combining intermittent fasting and veganism is so easy to try. Get started today and see how you feel!

Thank you for reading, I really enjoyed researching the topic and writing this book and hope it gives you the courage to take that first step and give it a try to hopefully improve your health and life like it has done mine!

Printed in Great Britain
by Amazon